KINGFISHER
READERS

level
1

Animal Colours

Thea Feldman

KINGFISHER

KINGFISHER

First published 2014 by Kingfisher
an imprint of Macmillan Children's Books
a division of Macmillan Publishers Limited
20 New Wharf Road, London N1 9RR
Basingstoke and Oxford
Associated companies throughout the world
www.panmacmillan.com

Series editor: Polly Goodman
Literacy consultant: Ellie Costa, Bank Street School for Children, New York
UK literacy consultant: Hilary Horton

ISBN: 978-0-7534-3662-2
Copyright © Macmillan Publishers Ltd 2014

9 8 7 6 5 4 3 2 1
1TR/0913/WKT/UG/115MA

J591.47

A CIP catalogue record for this book is available from the British Library.

Printed in China

Picture credits

The Publisher would like to thank the following for permission to reproduce their
material. Every care has been taken to trace copyright holders. However, if there
have been unintentional omissions or failure to trace copyright holders, we apologize
and will, if informed, endeavour to make corrections in any future edition.
Top = t; Bottom = b; Centre = c; Left = l; Right = r
Cover Steve Parish/Steve Parish Publishing/Corbis; 3 Shutterstock/chrom; 4 FLPA/Piotr Naskrecki/
Minden Pictures; 5 Shutterstock/Yellowj; 6t FLPA/Ingo Arndt/Minden Pictures; 6b Shutterstock; 7t; FLPA/
moomsabuy; 7b FLPA/Fabio Pupin; 8 FLPA/Michael Breuer/Biosphoto; 9 Shutterstock/Neale Cousland;
10t Shutterstock/Jason S; 10b Shutterstock/Mogens Trolle; 11t Shutterstock/Hung Chung Chih;
11b FLPA/Norbert Probst/Imagebroker; 12l Shutterstock/Serg64; 12r Shutterstock/Eric Isselee;
13t Shutterstock/Khoroshunova Olga; 13b Shutterstock/Eric Isselee; 14l Shutterstock/ romanvm66;
14c Shutterstock/Eric Isselee; 15t Shutterstock/bmaki; 15b Shutterstock/stockshotportfolio; 16–17 FLPA/
Alfred Schauhuber/Imagebroker; 18 Shutterstock/Eduard Kyslynskyi; 19 FLPA/Bernd Rohrschneider;
20 Shutterstock/Ian Grainger; 21 Shutterstock/Sue Robinson; 22 FLPA/Bernd Rohrschneider;
23 FLPA/Thorsten Negro/Imagebroker; 24t Shutterstock/Alfredo Maiquez; 24b Shutterstock/ Kletr;
25t Shutterstock/Brandon Alms; 25b Shutterstock/Dirk Ercken; 26 Shutterstock/Steve McWilliam;
27 Shutterstock/James Coleman; 28 FLPA/Thomas Marent/Minden Pictures; 29 Shutterstock/apiguide;
30t Shutterstock/worldswildlifewonders; 30bl FLPA/GTW/Imagebroker; 31t Shutterstock/Dobermaraner;
31b Shutterstock/Marty Wakat.

There are many colourful animals in the world!

This grasshopper is bright green.

This snake is green too.

These birds are pink.

This crab is red.
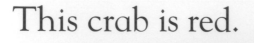

So is
this ant.

This starfish is blue.

So is this lizard.

This bear is brown
from its head to its tail.

It is all one colour.

Some animals are more than one colour.

How many different colours do you see on this bird?

Some animals are
black and white.

Some animals
have spots.

Some animals
have stripes.

The colours of some animals
help them hide from
other animals.

This is called **camouflage**
(say CAM-uh-flahj).

This brown **hare** hides from animals that hunt.

Its fur helps the hare **blend** in with the grass and the ground.

Do you see it?

A tiger is a hunter.

It has black and orange stripes.

A tiger's stripes help it hide in tall grass.

The tiger hides until
an animal comes near.

Then the tiger will jump
out to catch it!

Some animals change
their colour!

This spider is white
when it is on a white flower.

It turns yellow on a
yellow flower.
Insects do not see the spider.

The spider grabs and eats
this insect!

Sometimes this chameleon
(say ka-MEE-lee-yun)
is green.

Now it is red and white!

The chameleon can change colour in about 20 seconds.

The colours of some animals say "Stay away from me!"

These tiny frogs have **poison** in them.

Their bright
colours tell
other animals
"I taste bad!"

Other animals do not
eat the frogs.

The red on this moth lets other animals know it is not good to eat.

A skunk's white stripes
say "Go away!"

The colour of some animals helps them find **mates**.

This male lizard's orange neck says "Here I am!"

The bright colour helps female lizards find him.

This male peacock has bright tail feathers.

Females look for males with the brightest feathers.

Which colour
do you like
the best?

Can you find an animal that colour in this book?

Glossary

blend to mix in with other things of the same colour and be hard to see, such as a brown hare in front of earth or rocks

camouflage when an animal's colour helps it hide from other animals

hare a furry animal with long ears that looks a lot like a rabbit

mates animals that get together to have babies

poison something that some animals make that can kill other animals